Where Is Colorado?

Where Is Colorado?

by Jennifer Marino Walters

illustrated by Ted Hammond

Penguin Workshop

For Linda Mesward and the other wonderful NICU nurses at St. Francis Hospital in Colorado Springs. We will forever be grateful to you for taking such amazing care of our tiny twins!—JMW

PENGUIN WORKSHOP
An imprint of Penguin Random House LLC
1745 Broadway, New York, NY 10019
penguinrandomhouse.com

Designed and Produced by Dinardo Design, LLC.

Library of Congress Cataloging-in-Publication Data is available.

First published in the United States of America by Penguin Workshop, 2026

Manufactured in the United States of America
CJKW

ISBN 9798217244164 (paperback)
10 9 8 7 6 5 4 3 2 1

ISBN 9798217244171 (library binding)
10 9 8 7 6 5 4 3 2 1

The authorized representative in the EU for product safety and compliance is Penguin Random House Ireland, Morrison Chambers, 32 Nassau Street, Dublin D02 YH68, Ireland, https://eu-contact.penguin.ie.

Contents

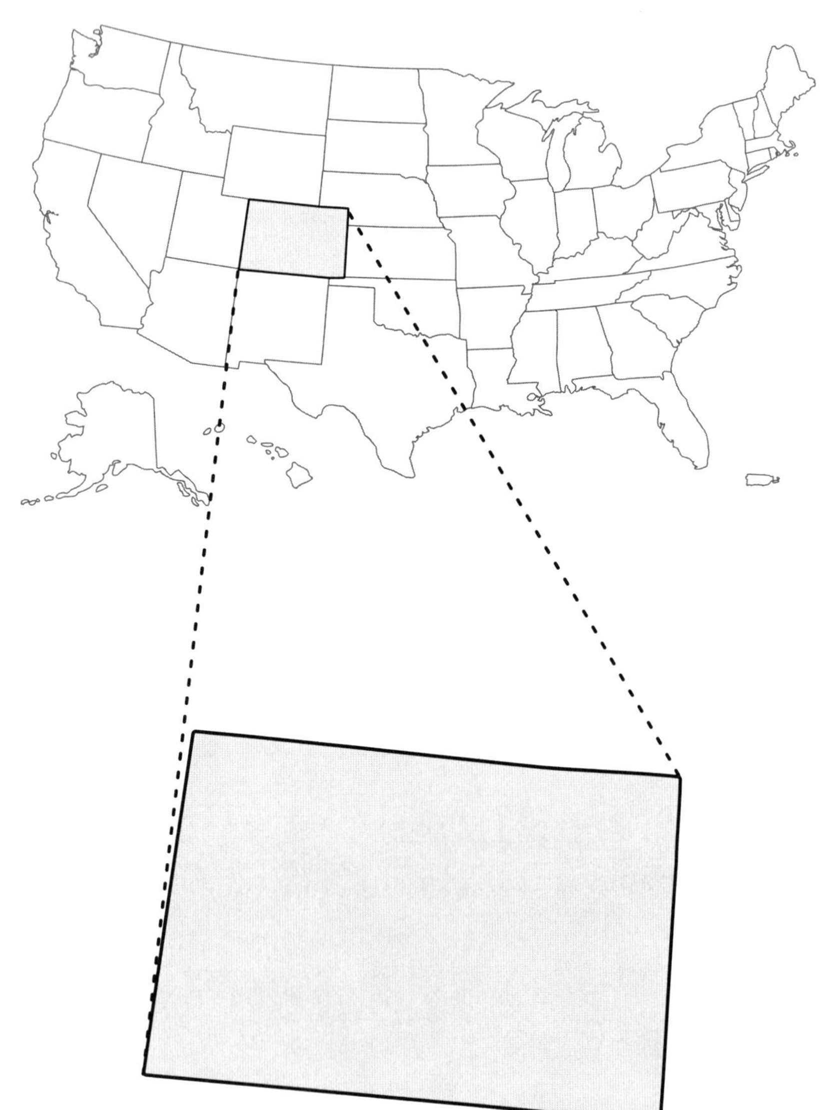

Where Is Colorado?

It was the summer of 1893. Katharine Lee Bates, a poet and professor at Wellesley College in Massachusetts, traveled to Colorado Springs. She would spend a few weeks there teaching English. One day, she and a group of fellow teachers rode a wagon to the summit of Pikes Peak. This famous mountain in the Rockies had already become a symbol of the American West.

Bates was in awe of the views from the peak. From its top, she could look out over the prairie grasses and wheat fields of Kansas! When she got back to her hotel, Bates wrote a poem. The first few lines, inspired by Pikes Peak, are as follows:

O beautiful for spacious skies,
For amber waves of grain,
For purple mountain majesties

Above the fruited plain!

Bates's poem was later set to music. It became the song "America the Beautiful." Colorado's mountains, and the land surrounding them, are still remembered through the song. They're a part of what many people picture when they think of Colorado today.

CHAPTER 1
Colorado's Land and Environment

Colorado is in the western United States. It is considered a Mountain state, even though only about half of it is in the Rocky Mountains. Colorado is bordered by Wyoming to the north, Nebraska to the northeast, Kansas to the east, Oklahoma to the southeast, New Mexico to the south, Arizona to the southwest, and Utah to the west. The spot where Arizona, Utah, Colorado, and New Mexico meet is called the Four Corners Monument. If someone lies down and spreads their arms and legs, they can be in four states at once!

Colorado is the eighth-largest US state by land area and the twenty-first most populous state. Its capital, Denver, is in the northern part of the state. It is Colorado's most populous city. The state got its name from the Colorado River, named by Spanish explorers because of the reddish color of its water (*colorado* means "colored red" in Spanish).

Colorado is known for the Rocky Mountains in the western part of the state. This mountain range stretches from New Mexico in the south to Canada in the north. The Colorado Plateau (say: plah-TOE) is also in the western part of Colorado. Eastern Colorado is full of grass-covered plains, while the north-central part of the state is home to the rolling, hilly Colorado Piedmont (say: PEED-mahnt). Colorado's elevation rises from roughly 3,350 feet in the east to over 14,000 feet in the west.

The eastern plains of Colorado are part of the Great Plains, a massive grassland covering over one million square miles in the center of North America. Corn and wheat are grown there, and cattle are raised there. Colorado's eastern plains tend to be dry. The major rivers there are the Arkansas and the South Platte (say: PLAT), which begin in the western mountains.

Prairie dogs, which are members of the squirrel family, live in Colorado's eastern plains. Prairie dogs have an advanced language. Through various squeals, chirps, squeaks, and other sounds, they give each other information about the size, shape, color, and speed of predators, such as rattlesnakes

and coyotes. Jackrabbits and antelope are also common in the eastern plains.

The Colorado Piedmont lies between the plains and the mountains and is about 50 miles wide and 275 miles long. Eighty percent of the state's population lives in the Piedmont, as do rabbits, raccoons, deer, coyotes, and other animals. The Piedmont is famous for its stunning red sandstone rock formations. The rocks formed over millions of years, when rivers and streams washed sediment (materials such as sand that is carried by water and wind) from the mountains. Over time, iron in the sand became exposed to oxygen and water, giving the rocks their red color.

One of the best places to see these red rocks is Garden of the Gods in Colorado Springs. Some of the rocks there are three hundred feet tall! Many have unique shapes that have given them interesting names. Balanced Rock, which balances on a small base, is a popular photo spot

for visitors (many of whom like to pretend they are holding up the rock).

The southern Rocky Mountains and the Colorado Plateau make up the western half of Colorado. There, mesas (flat-topped hills with steep sides) and mountain ranges stand among valleys and deep, narrow canyons. Various animals live in the Rocky Mountains, including bighorn sheep (Colorado's state animal), mountain lions,

black bears, and mountain goats.

Colorado's Rocky Mountains include several individual mountain ranges. The highest is the Sawatch Range in the center of the Rockies. It is home to Mount Elbert, Colorado's highest point at 14,440 feet. The San Juan (say: san hoo-ahn) Mountains are a volcanic plateau in the southwest that rises to over thirteen thousand feet. They contain the headwaters (beginning) of the Rio

Grande (say: REE-oh GRAND), one of North America's longest rivers. The north and northwest Rockies include the famous Front Range, home to Rocky Mountain National Park.

Rocky Mountain National Park was established in 1915. It contains dozens of mountains higher than twelve thousand feet, broad valleys and gorges carved by glaciers, and many lakes. The source of the Colorado River is in the northwestern corner of the park. The river flows west, traveling 1,450 miles through seven states and ending in the Gulf of California in Mexico. The Continental Divide runs through the center of Rocky Mountain National Park. The Continental Divide is a ridge of mountain peaks stretching from Canada, through four US states, and down into Mexico and Central America. It separates the continent's drainage into water that flows eastward to the Atlantic and the Gulf of Mexico and water that flows westward to the Pacific Ocean.

In total, Colorado has more than 830 peaks that are higher than eleven thousand feet in elevation. More than fifty of those peaks are fourteen thousand feet or higher and known as "fourteeners." Colorado is home to more fourteeners than any other state.

The Sangre de Cristo (say: SAHN-greh deh CRIS-toe) Mountains are in the south-central part of Colorado. They include Great Sand Dunes National Park and Preserve, one of four national parks in Colorado. Great Sand Dunes is home to the tallest sand dunes in North America. The tallest, Hidden Dune and Star Dune, are nearly 750 feet tall. Visitors can go sand sledding and sandboarding down the dunes! In the summer, they can also swim, float on a tube, or skimboard in Medano Creek. This creek forms at the base of the dunes from melting snow that flows down the mountains in the spring. By August, the creek starts to dry up.

Black Canyon of the Gunnison National Park in western Colorado contains some of the steepest cliffs and oldest rocks in North America. A canyon in the park, carved out by the Gunnison River over two million years, is 2,722 feet deep.

Mesa Verde (say: MAY-suh VEHR-day) National Park in southwest Colorado was the first national park created to protect human-made structures—about six hundred cliff dwellings built by Ancestral Pueblo (say: PWEH-blow) people in the late 1100s. The dwellings are made of sandstone, wood beams, and mud. Some of the walls are decorated with painted geometric patterns or petroglyphs (carvings) of animals, handprints, and other designs. The most complex of these dwellings—and the largest cliff dwelling in North America—is Cliff Palace. It has 150 rooms. Visitors can see Cliff Palace and other dwellings on ranger-led tours.

There are more than 1,500 lakes in Colorado.

Many of them are scattered throughout the mountains and fed by melted snow, making them cold throughout the year. But not all bodies of water in Colorado are cold. The state is also known for its hot springs! Hot springs form when rainwater or snowmelt seeps into cracks in the earth and meets hot rocks. The rocks heat the water, which then rises back to the surface and forms a spring. Springs throughout Colorado range from warm temperatures to burning hot. People soak in them to relax and soothe achy muscles. The world's largest hot springs pool is Glenwood Hot Springs. The town is even named after it: Glenwood Springs.

The climate of each area in Colorado depends largely on the elevation (how high it is above the ocean). In the eastern plains, it's warm in the summer and cold, dry, and windy in the winter. The Piedmont has a similar climate, and very hot days (above 90 degrees Fahrenheit) or very cold days (below 10 degrees Fahrenheit) are fairly common. The mountains and plateaus of western Colorado experience wide variations in temperature within short distances. The mountains are typically cold at higher elevations, while the lower plateaus and valleys can be 20 degrees warmer or more.

While Colorado is one of the top ten snowiest states in the country, average annual snowfall varies by elevation. For example, Denver—which has an elevation of about one mile (5,280 feet) above sea level—averages more than fifty-five inches of snow per year. The mountains, which can be nearly three times as high, sometimes get up to three hundred inches annually. That's because the higher the elevation, the colder the air, and colder air can hold less moisture. That moisture in the air instead forms ice crystals and falls as snow. At the same time, Colorado is one of the sunniest US states, with an average of over

250 days of sunshine per year!

Plant life also varies by elevation. The plains have mostly short grasses. The foothills of the Rocky Mountains, which range from 5,500 to 7,000 feet high, are full of oak, juniper, mountain mahogany, and pinyon pine trees. Pinyon pines produce pine nuts and can live up to one thousand years!

Ponderosa pines, Douglas firs, blue spruces, and aspen trees are found in areas that are about 7,000 to 11,500 feet in elevation. Aspen trees are known for their vibrant yellow leaves in the fall. Areas above 11,500 feet have very little plant life—mostly mosses and lichens (say: LYE-kins) that grow on rocks and wet ground.

CHAPTER 2
State Origins

Paleo-Indians lived in what is now Colorado as early as 13,000 BCE. Ancestral Pueblo Nations came to the Mesa Verde area around 550 CE. They set up cliff dwellings and complex farming systems. By the late 1200s, drought (say: DROWT) drove these Ancestral Pueblo people from their land. The Ute (say: YOOT) people settled in the southern Rocky Mountains by 1500.

In 1598, a group of Spanish explorers led by Juan de Oñate (say: hoo-ahn deh oh-NYAH-tay) entered the San Luis Valley, in the south-central part of what is now Colorado. These explorers were likely the first Europeans to set foot there. Oñate claimed the area as Spanish territory. In

Cliff dwellings at Mesa Verde today

1682, French explorers entered eastern Colorado. They claimed the land east of the Rocky Mountains for France.

The relationship between the Utes, the Spanish, and the French was sometimes peaceful and involved trading furs and other goods. Other times, there was conflict over land. The Arapaho (say: uh-RAP-uh-hoe) and Comanche (say: kuh-MAN-chee) Nations arrived in the 1700s and settled in the eastern plains.

In 1803, the United States bought the Louisiana Territory—land that stretched from the Mississippi River in the east to the Rocky Mountains in the west—from France. Even though there were already Indigenous peoples living in these areas, the United States acted as if it owned the land. This deal was known as the Louisiana Purchase. It included the eastern half of Colorado.

In 1806, the US Army sent a group of men

led by Lieutenant (say: loo-TEN-int) Zebulon Montgomery Pike to explore the southern part of the land the country received in the Louisiana Purchase and to find where the Arkansas and Red Rivers began. Over the course of several months, Pike and his group crossed present-day Kansas and entered what is now Colorado. Pike set up an outpost (a small military camp) near what we now call Pueblo, then headed northwest.

On November 15, Pike spotted what he described as "a small blue cloud" in the far distance. As he got closer, he realized it wasn't a cloud at all—it was a mountain! Pike called the mountain, which is part of the southern Front Range of the Rocky Mountains, Grand Peak. He greatly underestimated just how "grand" the mountain was. A few days later, Pike and three of his men set off to climb to the mountain's peak. They did not realize that it was over fourteen thousand feet tall! The group did not have the

proper clothing or supplies, and they encountered rough terrain and snowstorms. They were forced to turn back.

Despite his failure to make it to the top, Pike described the mountain in his journals, which he published. The mountain was later named Pikes Peak in his honor. Today, the 14,115-foot Pikes Peak is located near the city of Colorado Springs. Known as America's Mountain, Pikes Peak is a

symbol of the American West.

The first known person to reach the summit of Pikes Peak was Dr. Edwin James. He was part of a group of men led by explorer Stephen Long, who set out in 1820 to find the source of the Platte River. As Pike, Long, and other explorers spread knowledge of the Colorado area to fur traders, trappers, and others, more people came to see it. In some cases, Indigenous people, including the

Arapaho and Cheyenne (say: shy-ANN), helped guide them across the plains. Mexico ceded (gave up) a portion of Colorado to the United States in 1848 after the two-year Mexican-American War ended. And in 1850, the United States purchased the rest of Colorado from the Republic of Texas.

In 1858, gold was discovered near what is now downtown Denver. This sparked the Colorado Gold Rush. Over one hundred thousand people moved to Colorado in hopes of finding gold and becoming rich. They became known as Fifty-Niners because the gold rush peaked in 1859. Their motto was Pikes Peak or Bust. Many of them even painted those words on their wagons!

Mining camps, known as gold-dust towns, began to spring up in the mountains. The first permanent one was Gold Hill. Other big ones were Central City and Black Hawk. Some of the biggest cities in Colorado today, including Denver, Boulder, and Golden, began as mining

towns. At first, people panned gold from streams. Then they headed into the mountains to search for even more gold. But only a few gold seekers struck it rich before the gold rush ended in 1861, the year Colorado became a territory.

Even though the first rush had ended, people continued to move to Colorado to work in the mines. They began to fight more with the Indigenous people in the area—including the Ute, Cheyenne, Arapaho, and Comanche people—over their rights to land, water, and natural resources. The US government wanted Indigenous people to leave Colorado and move to other places to make room for the new settlers. Indigenous people wanted to stay where they had lived for so many generations.

On November 29, 1864, about 675 US troops launched a surprise attack on the peaceful Sand Creek camp in southeastern Colorado. They killed about 230 Arapaho and Cheyenne people, including women, children, and elderly people. Thirteen Cheyenne leaders and one Arapaho leader were also killed in the attack, which came to be known as the Sand Creek Massacre.

After the Sand Creek Massacre, the Little Arkansas Treaty of 1865 authorized the removal of the Arapaho and the Cheyenne people from Colorado. They were moved to reservations, or areas of land that are kept separate for Indigenous people to live on, mainly in Indian Territory (now Oklahoma). Representatives of the Arapaho and Cheyenne Nations signed the treaty because the United States promised to pay them for property that was stolen or destroyed during the Sand Creek Massacre and to give pieces of land to people who had lost loved ones in the attack. But the United States did not fulfill all its promises. The Comanche were also forced out of Colorado as more of their lands were taken over.

The building of railroads such as the Denver

Pacific Railroad, completed in 1870, brought even more settlers to Colorado. Colorado became the thirty-eighth US state in 1876. Around this time, silver was discovered in Leadville. This led to a silver boom, attracting even more people to work in silver mines.

Over the years, Colorado also attracted visitors. People heard about the beauty and dramatic scenery of the West and wanted to see it for themselves.

CHAPTER 3
Growth and Development

Because of this interest in Colorado, its population continued to increase. And as more people moved there, tensions with the Utes and other Indigenous nations continued to rise. Nathan Meeker was a federal agent for the White River Agency, which tried to assimilate Ute people (force them to give up their language, culture, and customs).

When soldiers trespassed on Ute land in northwest Colorado in September 1879, the Utes fought back. The six-day Battle of Milk Creek began. Meeker and about twenty other settlers were killed. Twenty-four Ute people were killed.

Congress passed the Ute Removal Act in 1880. This act authorized the forced removal of most

Ute groups in Colorado to reservations in Utah. The following year, nearly 1,500 Ute people were forced to leave their homes and move about 350 miles to these reservations. Only the Southern Ute people were allowed to stay on a reservation in southern Colorado.

In 1893, Colorado became only the second US state to give women the right to vote (Wyoming was the first). A year later, it elected three women to the Colorado House of Representatives. They were the first women to serve in any state legislature.

In the early 1900s, Colorado continued to grow thanks in part to the opening of US government

Clara Cressingham

Carrie Holly

Frances Klock

offices. One example is the Denver Mint, which opened in 1906. It's still open today! The Denver Mint can make 40,500 coins per minute, which adds up to millions of coins per day. Visitors can tour the mint and see coins being made.

The ski industry also began attracting people to the state. Colorado's first big ski resort, Winter Park, opened in 1940. It now has over 160 ski trails and slopes. Many others followed, and Colorado is now one of the top US states for skiing. Telluride, Steamboat, and Copper Mountain are some of the most popular ski resorts in Colorado today.

The US government also set up various military bases in Colorado during World War II (1939 to 1945). While the state was easily accessible, its location away from the coasts made it harder for enemies to attack it. The Rocky Mountain Arsenal opened in Commerce City in 1942 and was mainly used to make and store chemical weapons. Most of it is now a wildlife refuge. US Army base Camp Carson (now called Fort Carson) also opened in 1942 in Colorado Springs. That same year, the US Army opened Camp Hale, a training facility that's now a national historic site. Colorado Springs Army Air Base also opened that year. It was later named Peterson Air Force Base, then became Peterson Space Force Base in 2021.

These government and military projects attracted thousands of new residents to Colorado. By the late 1940s, only Washington, DC (the US capital), had more federal government offices than Colorado. Even after World War II, the US government continued to expand its presence. The US Air Force Academy opened in Denver in 1954 to train air force officers. It moved to Colorado Springs in 1958.

Colorado developed a strong aerospace industry in the mid-1950s. The aerospace industry designs, manufactures, and maintains aircraft and spacecraft. Two huge aerospace companies, Lockheed Martin and Ball Aerospace, opened in the state in 1956. North American Aerospace Defense Command (NORAD) opened in Colorado Springs in 1958. Its aim is to protect the United States and Canada from potential attacks by airplanes, missiles, and boats.

The Denver and Boulder areas also became a hub for technology companies. And in the 1970s, the Eisenhower-Johnson Memorial Tunnel opened. The tunnel allows drivers to travel through the Continental Divide at an average elevation of 11,112 feet, making it the highest automobile tunnel in the United States.

Colorado began to attract many top athletes in 1978, when the Colorado Springs Olympic & Paralympic Training Center opened. About fifteen thousand swimmers, figure skaters, wrestlers, and other athletes train there each year.

Training Up High

Colorado Springs was the perfect location for building the Olympic & Paralympic Training Center because of its elevation of over six thousand feet. The high elevation helps increase the flow of oxygen to athletes' muscles. That's because the air is thinner at high elevations, and thinner air contains less oxygen. The body is forced to produce more red blood cells, which carry oxygen. When the athletes return to lower elevations to compete, their bodies continue to carry more oxygen to their muscles, which can improve their performance.

The Olympic & Paralympic Training Center is open to the public for tours, during which visitors might get to see athletes training. Colorado Springs is also home to the US Olympic & Paralympic Museum, which opened in 2020. There, visitors can learn about some of America's greatest

Paralympic athletes practice sitting volleyball

athletes through interactive exhibits, displays, and artifacts. These include several athletes who were born in Colorado, such as Olympic alpine skier Mikaela Shiffrin and Paralympic wheelchair rugby player Josh O'Neill.

As Colorado welcomed more residents and visitors, its small airport could not handle all the incoming and outgoing travelers. In 1995, it was replaced with Denver International Airport (DIA). DIA is now the third-busiest airport in the United States and the sixth busiest in the world, with over eighty-two million passengers in 2024.

Denver gained even more national attention in August 2008, when it hosted the Democratic National Convention. During the convention, Barack Obama was nominated as the Democratic presidential candidate. He went on to win the 2008 election and became the first Black president of the United States.

CHAPTER 4
Today's State

Today, the Southern Ute Indian Tribe and the Ute Mountain Ute Tribe still live in Colorado on two reservations. More than one hundred thousand Indigenous people call Colorado home. Descendants of over two hundred Indigenous groups live in Denver, including the Cheyenne, Lakota, and Navajo. They are important to the culture and economy of their own communities, as well as to the state.

Agriculture is also important to Colorado's economy. Its major crops are corn, wheat, and hay. Colorado is one of the top cattle-producing states in the United States. Many hogs and sheep are raised there. The mining industry remains big. Northwestern Colorado has some of the country's largest coal deposits. Petroleum, gold, sand, and gravel are other important minerals.

Tourism and outdoor recreation are a huge part of Colorado's economy. In 2023 alone, the state had over ninety-three million visitors. Many are attracted to the state's huge ski resorts in Aspen, Vail, Breckenridge, and other places. They can also participate in other winter sports, including snowboarding, snow tubing, and snowshoeing.

Hiking is another popular outdoor activity in Colorado, with thousands of gorgeous trails throughout the state. Many of these trails are in the mountains. Rock climbing, white water rafting on the Arkansas and Colorado Rivers, kayaking, and camping are other popular outdoor activities.

Today, more than five hundred thousand people reach the summit of Pikes Peak each year. They don't all climb it! Some ride the Broadmoor

Manitou and Pikes Peak Cog Railway (the highest cog railway in the Northern Hemisphere, which opened for passenger service in 1891) to the peak. Others drive to the summit along the Pikes Peak Highway, a winding, nineteen-mile road with over 150 turns. The road was completed in 1915, following much of the same route as the old Pikes Peak Carriage Road, which once offered a wagon road to the summit.

Dinosaur lovers will also find lots to explore in Colorado. Dinosaurs roamed the area around 150 million years ago, and many fossils remain and continue to be discovered. Dinosaur National Monument is a nationally protected area in northwest Colorado that stretches into Utah. Visitors can get up close to over 1,500 dinosaur bones embedded in a rock wall and even touch some of them! The Denver Museum of Nature and Science and the Rocky Mountain Dinosaur Resource Center have giant dinosaur

skeletons on display. And the Dinosaur Journey Museum in western Colorado offers Dino Digs, where visitors can dig for actual dinosaur fossils alongside paleontologists (fossil scientists).

As in other western states, rodeos are popular in Colorado. A rodeo is a competition that shows off skills including bull riding and cattle roping. Cowboys and cowgirls from around the world come to Colorado each year to compete in rodeos

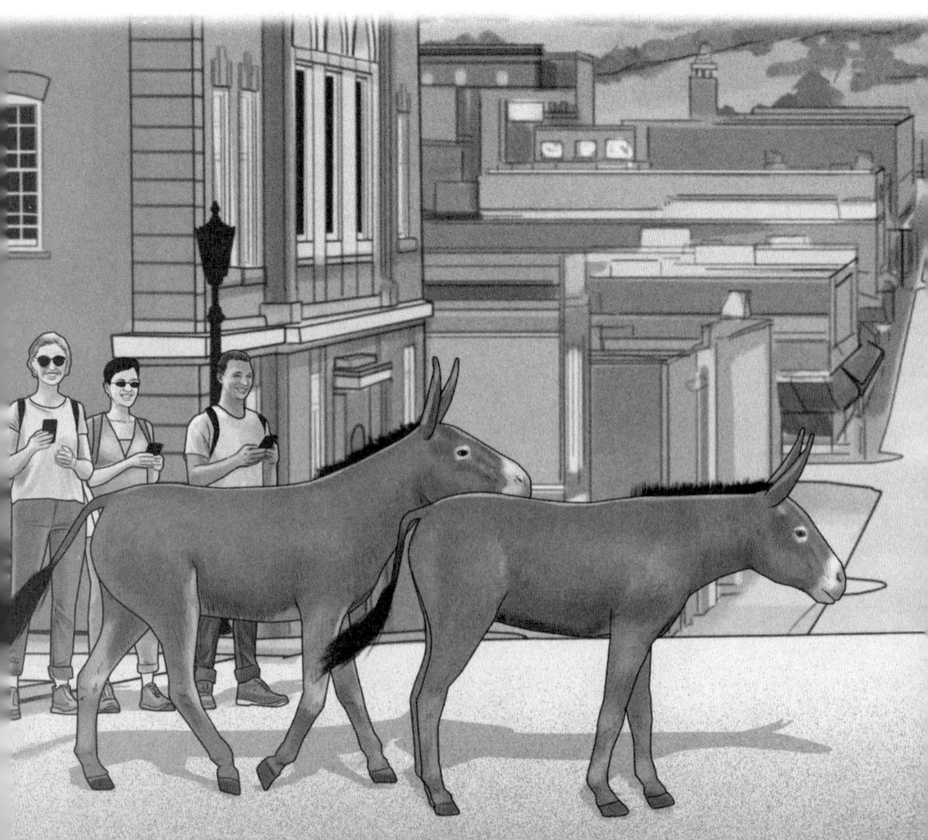

such as the Pikes Peak or Bust Rodeo, which takes place each July in Colorado Springs.

Many of Colorado's old gold-dust towns—some of which became ghost towns after the gold rush and later reopened—attract tourists, who enjoy the flavor of the Old West. Cripple Creek is famous for its herd of free-roaming donkeys, descendants of the burros (small donkeys) that once hauled ore from the mines.

Red Rocks Park and Amphitheatre, located in the foothills west of Denver, is a National Historic Landmark. Surrounded by red rocks, the natural amphitheater hosts frequent concerts and festivals. The Central City Opera House, open since 1878, presents operas and other shows. The Colorado Symphony Orchestra and various theater, opera, and ballet companies perform at the Denver Performing Arts Complex. The Denver Art Museum displays works of art from all over the world. Its collection includes paintings from Peru, sculptures and jewelry from Africa, ceramics from Japan, and so much more.

Colorado has one of the highest numbers of college graduates among all US states. There are also more than forty colleges and universities in the state. The University of Colorado opened in 1876 in Boulder. It has three other campuses, including Colorado Springs, Denver, and Anschutz Medical Campus. Colorado State

University in Fort Collins opened in 1870, and the Colorado School of Mines in Golden was founded in 1874.

Several professional sports teams play in Colorado. All of them are based in Denver. The National Football League's Denver Broncos won the Super Bowl three times—in 1998 and 1999 under star quarterback John Elway, and again in 2016. The National Hockey League's Colorado Avalanche moved to Denver from Quebec, Canada, in 1995 and have won the Stanley Cup three times. And the Denver Nuggets won their first National Basketball Association championship in 2023. Major League Baseball's Colorado Rockies and Major League Soccer's Colorado Rapids also play in Denver.

Besides "America the Beautiful," many other songs have been inspired by the beauty of Colorado, such as "Denver" by Willie Nelson and "Colorado" by Florida Georgia Line. Singer-songwriter John Denver loved Colorado and the Rocky Mountains so much that he even named himself after the city of Denver! John Denver wrote many songs about the state. One of them, "Rocky Mountain High," became one of Colorado's official state songs.

From the grassy plains of eastern Colorado to the majestic, often snow-capped mountains in the west, Colorado is a breathtaking state, still known for its dramatic and striking landscapes.

Colorado at a Glance

Statehood: 1876

Nickname: The Centennial State

Abbreviation: CO

State Motto: *Nil sine numine* (Latin for "Nothing without providence")

State Tree: Colorado blue spruce

State Animal: Rocky Mountain bighorn sheep

Capital: Denver

Size: 104,094 square miles

Population: About 6 million

Famous People from Colorado: Christian McCaffrey (NFL running back), Kristin Davis (actor), Neil Gorsuch (US Supreme Court justice), India Arie (musician)

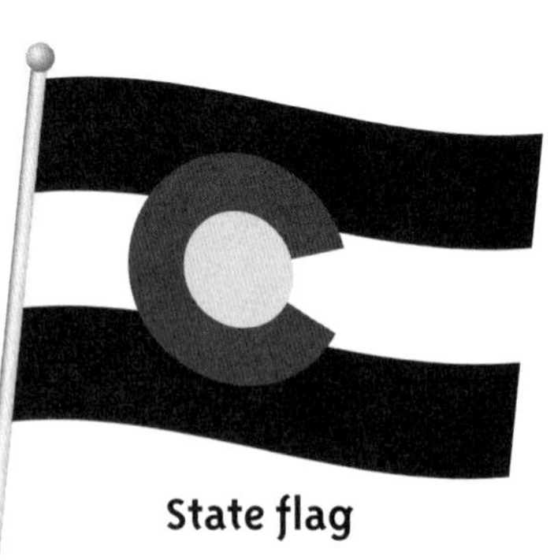

State flag

State bird
Lark bunting

State flower
Columbine

FUN FACT:

Denver is known as the Mile High City because it is one mile (or 5,280 feet) above sea level. While not all of the city is at that exact elevation, the thirteenth step of the Colorado State Capitol is. A plaque on the step serves as the official mile-high marker.

Timeline of Colorado

1190s	Ancestral Puebloans build cave dwellings in what is now Mesa Verde
1598	Spanish explorer Juan de Oñate enters southern Colorado and claims the area for Spain
1682	French explorers arrive in eastern Colorado and claim the land east of the Rocky Mountains for France
1806	Zebulon Montgomery Pike discovers Pikes Peak
1848	Mexico cedes most of Colorado to the United States
1858	The Colorado Gold Rush begins
1876	Colorado becomes the thirty-eighth US state
1906	The Denver Mint opens
1915	Rocky Mountain National Park is established
1940	Colorado's first big ski resort, Winter Park, opens
1954	The US Air Force Academy opens in Denver
1978	The Colorado Springs Olympic & Paralympic Training Center opens
1995	Denver International Airport opens
2008	The Democratic National Convention takes place in Denver
2023	The Denver Nuggets win their first NBA championship

Timeline of the World

1588 — The English defeat the Spanish Armada

1687 — Sir Isaac Newton describes his theory of gravity

1807 — Britain bans the slave trade

1821 — Mexico gains independence from Spain

1848 — The California Gold Rush begins

1858 — The first telegraph is sent by transatlantic cable

1869 — The Suez Canal opens in Egypt, connecting the Mediterranean Sea to the Red Sea

1879 — Albert Einstein is born

1893 — New Zealand becomes the first country to give women the right to vote

1912 — The *Titanic* sinks after hitting an iceberg

1954 — Elvis Presley releases his first single, "That's All Right"

1976 — North and South Vietnam are united

1981 — MTV airs its first music videos

1994 — Nelson Mandela becomes the first Black president of South Africa

2010 — The Burj Khalifa in Dubai opens and becomes the tallest building in the world

2023 — India surpasses China as the world's most populous country

Bibliography

***Books for young readers**

*Meinking, Mary. ***What's Great About Colorado?*** Minneapolis, MN: Lerner Publishing Group, 2014.

*Zeiger, Jennifer. ***Colorado.*** A True Book: My United States. New York: Scholastic Children's Press, 2017.

Websites

The Broadmoor Manitou and Pikes Peak Cog Railway: www.cograilway.com

Great Sand Dunes National Park and Preserve: www.nps.gov/grsa/index.htm

Mesa Verde National Park: www.nps.gov/meve/index.htm

Rocky Mountain National Park: www.nps.gov/romo/index.htm